Animal Lives

WILD HORSES

Sally Morgan

QEB Publishing

Published in the United States by
QEB Publishing, Inc.
23062 La Cadena Drive
Laguna Hills, CA 92653

www.qeb-publishing.com

Library of Congress Control Number: 2008011527

ISBN 978 1 59566 539 3

Written by Sally Morgan
Design and editorial by East River Partnership

Publisher Steve Evans
Creative Director Zeta Davies

Printed and bound in the United States

Picture Credits

Key: t = top, b = bottom, l = left, r = right,
c = center, FC = front cover

Corbis /Corbis 7tr, /Kit Houghton 8–9, /Steven
G. Smith 14–15, /Frans Lemmens/zefa 18–19;
Getty /Art Wolfe 24–25; **Photolibrary** /Juniors
Bildarchiv 10, /Animals Animals 5bl, /Animals
Animals 23; **Photoshot/NHPA** /Henry Ausloos
16, /Martin Harvey 26, /Anthony Bannister 27,
/Ernie Janes 28–29; **Shutterstock** /Webtrias 1,
/Winthrop Brookhouse 4br, 4–5, /Judy Worley
6–7, /Marilyn Barbone 11, /Winthrop Brookhouse
12–13, /Ovidiu Iordachi 12l, /Lincoln Rogers
15t, /Rodney Mehring 17, /Medvedev Vladimir
19tl, /Roman Barelko 20–21, /Lior Filshteiner
20tr, /Winthrop Brookhouse 21tr, /Winthrop
Brookhouse 22, /Eleanor 25tl, /Jeanne Hatch
28br, /RTImages 30r, /Winthrop Brookhouse
30m, /Winthrop Brookhouse 30l, /Trutta55
background image 2–3, 10–11, 16–17, 22–23,
26–27, 30–31, 32.

Words in **bold** are explained in
the glossary on page 31.

Contents

The wild horse

Wild horses were first tamed by people thousands of years ago. Today, although many of the world's horses have been tamed, there are still some running wild.

Barrel-shaped bodies

Horses are swift-moving, four-legged animals that are related to zebras and donkeys. They have a barrel-shaped body, a **mane** down their neck, and a short tail with very long hairs.

Mustang herds roam free in parts of the North American west.

A young foal stays close to its mother, the mare.

Mammals

The horse is a type of **mammal**. This means that female horses give birth to live young and feed them with their milk. Like most other mammals, including gorillas and lions, horses have hair covering their body.

Stallions, mares, and foals

A male horse is called a stallion and a female is a mare. A newborn horse is known as a foal. Horses are social animals and prefer to live in groups called herds.

A stallion, or male horse, is usually larger than a mare.

Horse types

There is only one true wild horse left in the world; all others are now **extinct**. This is the Przewalski's horse from **Mongolia**. Przewalski's is pronounced psher-VAHL-skeez.

Spirit horse

The Mongolians call the Przewalski's horse 'takhi,' which means 'spirit.' This horse got its name because it is so fierce that it is impossible to ride. Mongolians believe that no one has ever been able to ride a Przewalski's horse other than Genghis Khan, the famous Mongol leader who lived 800 years ago.

Wild horse fact!

Mustangs come from Spanish horses that were taken to Mexico from Spain. Many were taken by Native Americans, who then bred from them.

6

Australia's wild horse, the brumby, has a large head and short neck and back.

Feral horses

There are other wild horses in the world, but these are **descended** from horses that escaped from **captivity** to roam free. This type of horse is called a **feral** horse. For example, there are mustangs in the United States, brumbies in Australia, and sorraia horses in Spain. New Forest ponies roam wild in the New Forest region of the United Kingdom.

The mane of a Przewalski's horse stands upright.

Where do you find wild horses?

Wild horses used to be found across Europe and Asia, from Poland to Mongolia. A wild horse called the Tarpan once ran free across central Asia, but is now extinct. The Przewalski's horse roamed across Mongolia and Northern China and lived on the dry grasslands and **deserts**, which were extremely cold in winter. Today, the Przewalski's horse is protected and runs free in smaller numbers in special areas of Mongolia.

Wetlands and grasslands

Feral horses live in the Camargue, a wetland area in southern France. Mustangs live on dry grassland in central and western parts of the United States. The brumbies of Australia live on the dry, central grasslands, while the Kaimanawa horse lives on the North Island of New Zealand.

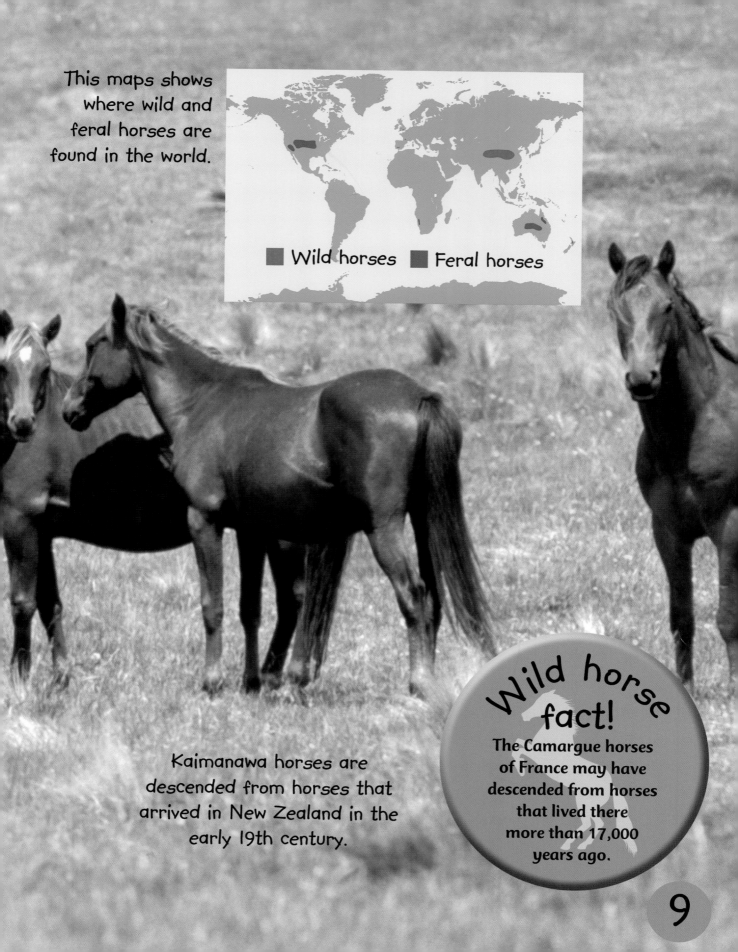

This maps shows where wild and feral horses are found in the world.

■ Wild horses   ■ Feral horses

Kaimanawa horses are descended from horses that arrived in New Zealand in the early 19th century.

Wild horse fact!
The Camargue horses of France may have descended from horses that lived there more than 17,000 years ago.

9

Beginning life

Mares are ready to breed when they are two to three years old. After a stallion and a mare mate, the mare is **pregnant** for about a year before giving birth to one foal, or occasionally twins.

Born at night

Most foals are born at night when it is dark and there is less chance of being seen by **predators**. A newborn foal can stand and walk after an hour. It soon begins drinking its mother's milk. At about one week old, the foal's first teeth begin to appear and it can nibble grass.

Camargue foals are born black or brown, but they start to turn white at about four years of age.

Milk hair

A young foal has soft, woolly hair, which is often called 'milk hair.' The foal loses this hair when it is about two months old. The milk hair is replaced by longer, coarser hair.

Following mum

Newborn foals follow their mother closely for the first few days. The mother is very protective and will use her hooves to attack any animal that comes too close.

Wild horse fact!

Mares hardly ever give birth to twin foals. It is also very rare for twin foals to survive in the wild.

A foal's legs are almost as long as those of a fully grown horse.

Growing up

The foal feeds on its mother's milk and nibbles grass for about seven months. After it is **weaned** and stops drinking its mother's milk, the foal feeds only on grass and other plants. At nine months, it has a full set of teeth, which are called milk teeth. By the time it is five or six years old, the foal's milk teeth have fallen out and its adult teeth have grown.

By the time it is five years old, a horse may have up to 44 teeth.

Colts and fillies

A young male foal is called a colt until his fourth birthday. He then becomes a stallion. A female foal is called a filly until she is four years old, when she becomes a mare. Horses grow until they are five to ten years old. As they get older, their body slowly gets larger and they begin to appear less 'leggy.'

You can tell the age of a horse from a groove on one of its front teeth. The groove first appears when the horse is 10 years old. By 15 years, the groove stretches halfway down its tooth.

Young horses may nip each other with their teeth during play. This is all part of growing up.

13

Living in herds

Wild horses live in groups called herds. A herd is made up of one or two stallions and up to ten mares and their foals. One of the mares, called the lead mare, leads the herd and decides where it will **graze**. It is the job of the stallions to watch and protect the herd from predators.

Wild horse fact!

The Przewalski's horse is named after the Russian explorer Nikolai Przewalski. He discovered these horses in the 1870s.

Young stallions often fight for their place in the herd.

The lead mare guides
the herd to graze.

eaving the herd

llies and colts stay with their herd until
ey are two years old. The stallions
en force them to leave. The fillies join
her herds and the colts get together
ith other colts to form a **'bachelor'**
oup. When a colt is older, it may try
take over a herd of mares by fighting
ith the herd's stallion. Stallions fight
ing their teeth and hooves.

Grazing grass

Wild horses are **herbivores**, or animals that eat plants. Horses mostly graze on grass, but will also eat the leaves and fruits of other plants, and even tree bark and the buds of shrubs.

Walking and eating

Horses graze as they walk. They take a few steps, eat some grass, and then move on a couple of steps. When there is a lot of good grass, horses only spend a few hours eating. If there is only a little grass, or it is too dry, a horse may have to graze for 22 hours a day in order to get enough food.

In winter, Camargue horses survive on dried grass and goosefoot. This is a tough plant that most other grazing animals cannot eat.

Teeth for grazing

A horse's teeth are designed for grazing on grass. The small teeth at the front of their mouth nip off blades of grass, while the large, flat teeth at the back grind up the tough grass. Lots of chewing rubs the tops of the teeth, so an old horse may have teeth that are worn right down to the roots.

A horse uses its tongue to push grass onto its back teeth to be chewed.

Desert horses

Some wild horses can survive in deserts where there is very little grazing and water. The brumbies of the deserts of central Australia and the wild horses of the Namib Desert in Namibia, for example, live in extremely dry areas.

Wild horse fact!

Namib horses produce dry **dung** that is rich in fat. Fat is a good source of energy, so the horses eat their own dung. They absorb the fat as it passes through their gut.

Long distances

Desert horses feed on the tough grasses that grow in the desert. During the dry months of the year, they walk long distances each day to find water holes from which to drink. When it rains they stay in one place. These horses often feed at night, when it is much cooler.

Namib Desert horses walk long distances each day in search of grass and water.

Cold deserts

The Gobi Desert of Mongolia is dry but very cold in winter. To protect themselves against this cold, Przewalski's horses have thick coats. During sand storms, they turn their back to the wind and tuck their tail tightly between their back legs. This helps to protect the rest of their body from the sand.

Przewalski's horses use their sharp hooves to dig through the soil to reach water in the ground.

Horse senses

Horses have excellent senses that they use to find food and to spot predators.

Eyes, ears, and nose

A horse's large, wide-apart eyes are set high on its head. This means that it can see most of the way around and watch out for predators. A horse also has large ears, which it can swivel easily. This allows it to work out the direction from which a sound is coming. A horse's good sense of smell also helps it to detect danger.

Horses cannot see directly behind them without turning their heads.

Horses protect themselves from danger by using their senses of hearing and smell.

eeling vibrations

lorses are able to feel vibrations
n the ground through their
ooves. This means that they
an tell when other animals are
noving around quite far away.
lorses can do this even though
ney cannot see or hear them.

Wild horses
need to stay
alert so that
they can hear
other animals
approaching.

Wild horse
fact!

Horses have two blind spots,
or places where they are not
able to see. They cannot see
anything behind them or
anything in front, just
below their nose.

21

Horse movement

A horse always has two or three hooves on the ground when it walks. First it moves a **foreleg** forward, then the **hind leg** on the same side. This is followed by the other foreleg and hind leg.

A horse canters at between 10 and 15 miles an hour.

Hind leg

Foreleg

Trotting and cantering

When trotting, which is faster than walking, a horse moves one foreleg and the opposite hind leg forward at the same time. When cantering, a horse moves one foreleg forward, then the other foreleg and opposite hind leg at the same time, and finally the other hind leg.

Galloping

Horses gallop, or run, if they need to escape from danger. When galloping, they lift their hind legs together and move these forward. Then they do the same with their forelegs.

When one horse sits down, others stand and watch for predators.

Sitting to sleep

Horses can sleep standing up or sitting down. But they are most at risk from attack by predators when sitting down. For example, wolves may attack sleeping mustangs.

23

Home range

Many herds live in an area called a home range. Horses in a herd find all the food and water they need in this area. Some stallions mark the edge of their home range by dropping their dung in piles along the **boundary**. Stallions of neighboring herds do not fight over land, but they may fight over mares.

Nomadic herds

Some herds are nomadic. This means they do not have a home range. Instead, they keep on moving in search of food. They may move to particular areas at certain times of the year when they know there will be plenty of grass to eat.

A small herd of Przewalski's horses grazes a grassy hillside.

Night and day

Horses spend much of the day walking around and eating. At some point during the day, the herd will walk to a water hole or river to drink. At night, the herd gathers close together and the horses sleep for a few hours.

Australian brumbies roam over wide areas to find good grazing.

Wild horse fact!

The name 'brumby' may have come from the Aboriginal word 'baroomby,' which means 'wild.' A group of brumbies is called a mob!

Communication

Horses communicate using sounds, touch, and smell. They can make many sounds, including **whinnies**, squeals, and shrill cries. They also gently nuzzle and groom each other. Horses use their front teeth to clean those areas of another horse's coat, such as the shoulders and back, that are difficult to reach.

Grooming calms horses and strengthens their friendships.

Body language

Horses can also communicate by using parts of their body. The position of the ears is a signal to other horses. For example, flattened ears is a sign that a horse is angry. The way a horse swishes its tail is important, too, and lets other horses know if the horse is feeling angry or anxious.

The horse on the left has its ears back and may be threatening the other horse.

Wild horse fact!

Scientists have found that when horses groom each other on the back of their neck, their heart beats more slowly.

27

Wild horses under threat

In 1968, the Przewalski's horse disappeared from the wild. This was because it was hunted by people, and the grasslands where it lived were used for grazing cattle. Fortunately, some Przewalski's horses survived in zoos where they were bred successfully. Some have now been returned to Mongolia and released into special grasslands where they are protected from hunters.

About 50,000 mustangs now live in the wild in North America.

Przewalski's horses that were born in zoos have to learn how to live in the wild.

Saving wild horses

Feral horses are under threat, too. Lots of these horses have lost their **habitat** to farming, and many have been captured and used for riding. In the past, for example, many mustangs were caught and used by the United States Army. Now, however, free-roaming horses on public land are protected in the United States.

Life cycle of a wild horse

A mare is ready to breed when she is two to three years old. She is pregnant for up to one year. Mares usually have one foal every two years. Wild horses live for 20 to 25 years in the wild, although a few have lived to 30 years of age. The oldest kept horse was 62 years old.

Newborn foal

Older foal

Adult

Glossary

bachelor (in horses) male horse that lives with other males

boundary edge of a territory

captivity when animals are kept and cared for by people

descended come by birth from a certain animal or family group

desert a dry place that gets very little rain. Some deserts are hot, but others are cold places

dung the droppings of an animal

extinct no longer in existence, disappeared completely

feral animals that have escaped from captivity and are living wild

foreleg front leg

graze to feed on grass and other plants

habitat the place in which an animal or plant lives

herbivore an animal that eats plants

hind leg back leg

mammal an animal that gives birth to live young, rather than laying eggs. Female mammals produce milk to feed their young

mane the thick hair that grows along the top of the neck of a horse

Mongolia a country in Central Asia

predator an animal that hunts other animals

pregnant describes a female animal that has a baby, or babies, developing inside her

weaned when a young animal starts to eat solid food rather than just drinking its mother's milk

whinny neighing sound made by a horse

Index